Skipping Rocks

Skipping Rocks

A lifetime of lines and verse

Susan Shultz

We write to taste life twice
- Anaïs Nin

For Lucy Jane and Annabelle Lee.

Unworthy Trustee

A second hand kneeler
For Emily

My mouth twists in laughter
For Dorothy

The saint and the sinner
To both I could talk

One who worships the cardinal
And the other the hawk

My sisters in words
So different yet same

Both danced near their losses
Both fearless of flame

May I introduce you
Parker and Dickinson

I carry their burden
Their poisoned pen

I sit at their table
Dichotomy bound

But you know no one else
Will be buying this round

A second hand kneeler
But I have two knees

And give humble tribute
— Their unworthy trustee

Fireflies

August and the fireflies are gone —
Free from those who'd seize their light.
Your jars can't capture childhood, air tight.
The darkness a reminder until the dawn.

The dusk now has a welcome cool,
But we are never satisfied.
Long for the heat, long for the fall —
With its bees and angsty school
Perhaps a Halloween ghoul.

The fireflies are gone
And we lament,
forced to move on
Proceed our flight's descent.

Their flash, a slow beat —
A soft, vulnerable heat.
Death a thumb's fluorescent streak —
A century of children need to seek.

Their sole purpose –
To Light your night
Amuse you with their random, oddball sight
The dusk has a welcome cool.

But we are never satisfied

The fireflies are gone
And only darkness is left behind.
Are they free – or has fate dissolved their stars?
All we can do is try to fight our jars.

The Music is Mine

And the dream comes again
Opens my heart
To release a thousand doves
In a flurry of white wings
They carry me
To a world of blue sky
And weightlessness

And the dream lives again
Fills me with light
And takes away my sorrow
I dance with the angels
And the music is yours

And so I can live again
Though I wake
To a world that is heavy
My heart is filled
With a thousand white doves
Waiting to carry me
To a world of blue sky
Weightlessness
And you

And the music is mine.

Everything I save gets thrown away

Everything I save gets thrown away
No matter where I tuck it, it can't stay
I don't keep everything, just bits of clay
That make up who I am, in effigy

It's not like I keep idols on display
A root I save to grow another day
Newspapers now forgotten, fade away
My dusty hands are earnest when they pray

I know what I should save and what can't stay
Mostly inside my heart, where memories lay
I don't scrapbook, organize, fillet
My memories, in frying pan sauté

Leftovers that I'd rapidly misplace
So my deliberate archive is the way
To mentally decide what I should save
To choose what my sad legacy may say

But everything I save gets thrown away
The bulbs I dug out after garden's prime
Now lost to basements, bad luck and time

I guess my ultimate legacy will lay

Despite my efforts, in your hearts, I pray
Please let it grow there — a stable, sweet soufflé
Since everything I save gets thrown away

It's my own fault, as I can't seem to see
What matters more is saving what's in me

The Moonchild

Cradled in the darkest shades of blackness
lies my moon.
Vividness that never fades
Drifts all around my room.

The shadow that she finds me in
Are quickly chased away.
The glow that I am drenched in
Mocks even the light of day.

The child of its cooling beauty,
Soothed by evening skies —
Reflect the flower of her center
Deep within my nightlike eyes.

When the heat of desperation
Finally sets with Brother Sun —
Feel the freedom of the Moonchild.
We, in darkness, dance as one.

The Mason Jar

If you don't have a Mason jar,
Your life's gone astray —
A candle, a vase,
Or artsy Chardonnay.

Love, steamed and sealed
By hands, young, or the wrinkled —
Preserves your preserves
And brines the ass off your pickle.

An image of warmth
And Gifts made for eating —
Ye old Mason jar
Makes food much less fleeting.

You boil, I'll bake
You jam, I'll ribbon
The Mason jar means
All old angst's forgiven

The country fair's hero,
The firefly's woe,
The scrambled egg shaker,
Decay's foremost foe.

A bread or a cake,
A soup or a crop,
A salad to shake,
Just don't let it drop.

If you get a Mason jar
Keep it tight, undisrupted.
Then you clean, pass it on
You'll gift joy uncorrupted.

The summer tomato, warms a cold winter supper.
It's sugared strawberry uplifts plain toast and butter.
Its cocktail looks wholesome, humble, and sweet —
Despite width and depth knocking you off your feet.

Inside its confines, spells and secrets airtight
Then its treasures will yield , with the tip of your knife.
The first line of defense of love's labor worth giving
The pop of the top honors past, new beginnings

If you don't have a Mason jar
Your life's gone astray —
Because surely there's kindness
It's time to repay.

A Painless Euthanasia

A love I'd kept
Died yesterday
As silently
As sleep.

A painless euthanasia
There was no need to weep

No one came
And mourned it
As I held it, still and cold.

So all alone,
I buried it —
My churchyard, vast and old.

Service Roads

I always choose the service road
If I have time to spare
I get more life that's picturesque
And skip the speed and tear

I don't mind the stop sign or two
The traffic light that slows
I'd rather see what I pass through
Than feel the road rage blows

The country diner, sketchy dive
The thrift shop that I'd love
Lest I'd be flying 65
Switching lanes, and push and shove

The road less traveled, service lane
Slow down, less stress, less worry
Unless you find the Bates motel
And end in taxidermy

A Distant Highway

I do not know
This woman that silently speaks to me.
Calls to me in black and white
A thousand words
From twisted metal.
We've never met
There is no
Explanation
Consolation.

I cry for her life
Gaping holes
In various circles
The howling wind
Whistling
From a distant highway.

I cry for her children
Their only hope
To see love in others
Rebuilding the dreams
Crushed in twisted metal
On a distant highway.

Hands

I'm so hard on my body
but ok with my hands.
My eyes see they're flawed
but my head understands.

I don't worry they're aged
or if they show years.
I know they've absorbed
a thousand dried tears.

They show my frailty
in long-bitten nails.
Share the scars from those times
I chose heads but got tails.

They have the signs
of my work in the kitchen
They bear the lines of a life
that's been lived in.

The finders of every
lost precious stuffed teddy.
Hair brushers, night soothers
and butterers of spaghetti.

My nails are more likely
to brandish the soil.

Of planting and weeding,
the gardener's toil.

They've no manicure,
and no cuticle trim.
No filler, no tips,
and no paraffin.

Purveyors of words that
my lips can't expel
Stained with ink, keyboard-calloused,
they backspace, and misspell.

The transmitters of heart
and the agents of brain.
The symbols of peace,
the easers of pain.

 A gypsy would find
my palms' tales confusing.
Won't find fortune or fame,
but the lifeline's amusing.

Undying Devotion

Devotion that's undying is a frightening sort of fate
For, aptly named, it weakens not, nor quiets in the night
Immortal and unending love, that's always within sight
The very polar opposite of deepest vengeful hate

Undying, not eternal, which implies an ebb and flow
Though constant, not intense, as that which can't begin to die
The pounding of a mother's heart, the tears the martyrs cry
The spillage of a soldier's blood, a sacrificial show

You hold the power to evoke what you need me to be
I'll mold and shape to fit your hand, fill any empty space
And in return, this beggar asks for any spare embrace
A coin or two of love from you — past that small price, I'm free

Devotion that's undying is a fate that I accept.
It lives on in these words that tell of secrets that we've kept.

I Drunk Dialed Jesus

I drunk dialed Jesus
And he hit ignore.
I'm sure he expected
What he's heard before.

I drunk dialed Jesus –
But I knew he'd not care
Because it's been so long
Since he'd answered my prayer.

I drunk dialed Jesus
To bring up the 80s –
And he rolled his eyes
And said, "covered that, lady."

I drunk dialed Jesus –
Used kneeler and tears –
Begged for forgiveness
For so many years

I tried to explain.
Why I'd made these mistakes.
His glasses of stain
Made my broken heart ache.

I drunk dialed Jesus

On hold, soul a drift
Maybe he's
Trying to get me a Lyft

Insomnia

I have grown weary of these bones.
They are sponges, soaking the tainted
Blood that spills from my torn heart,
Blood that aches, polluted by pain.

I'd thought I'd found some reprieve.
But I struggle, only
To find I'm deeper than ever
In this quiet quicksand.

I long for the beginnings of decay
And the earth embraces my longing
And welcomes me home —
To be broken down into
The elements that make me
Foul in their composition
But perfect in their separation.

Like the water, I will be crystal clear
And part of every living thing.

I will be everywhere
I will be like the wind
Unable to be caught
In these frightened days
And lonely and sordid nights.

The wind knows no end or beginning.
It tosses the tattered pieces of my life.
And haunts the empty halls of my heart
Making a low whistling sound....

If I don't laugh
I'm afraid you'll hear it
In the silence.

March

The earth is slowly stirring in the sun
That's growing warmer with each passing day
I wake to songbirds heralding the dawn
Trees stretch their limbs to shake the snow away

The arms of sky are welcoming and blue
As life stops walking and begins to run
Though starting slowly, my heart races too
My own rebirth, renewal, just begun

The cycles turning are not without pain
I thrust myself from darkness into light
My eyes, my body will reflect the strain
As deep within, my very natures fight

Don't worry if I shudder in the cold
I'm waiting for the spring to thaw my soul

Wind

Oh, that wind.

Rips down our dry tree tops
Knocks out our weak power

Rips off our last leaves.
Whistles through creepy eaves.
Won't give fall a reprieve.

Oh, that wind.

Makes our clouds slowly dance.
Teases white foam from surf.
Gives the butterflies a chance.

Oh, that wind.

Fills my starved lungs with air.
Carries upward my prayer,

Makes me feel my wings are there.

Hummingbird

Flutter —
Unbelievable
Unattainable

My soul
With long-sought wings
You flutter
barely in sight —
delicate and determined
swayed by sugar.

That glimpse of heaven
Tiny, trembling, tenacious
Wings, like an angel's tears

A temporary traveler —
A sneaking spirit.
A miraculous wisp that seems to —

Flutter,
my cheeky cherub —
my flickering heart —
my fleeting friend.
Until your wings
can lift my soul
again.

The Change

I taste the blood
My wasted blood.
I block the flood
This messy mud.

It just won't stay.
My brain's ok.
My flag is waving —
It's not worth saving.

I mourn my youth
But don't miss pain —
Accept the truth
That comes again.

It's not given
What it should have.
All I'd hoped
Was that it would have.

I have these parts
These painful sacks —
But now it's time
To give them back.

I see this blood
This aged warning.

From my gut —
My hollow mourning.

The deepest thing that gives me pause —
My hardest labor — menopause.

Blackberry

No love like a blackberry
Sweet but still sour
I reach for your treasures
Then pick thorns for an hour

Your berries, they stain
My mouth and my skin
Water you with the blood
You've drawn from within

I tamed you, blackberry
I wrestled fanged vines
Until your sharp tendrils
Find more fences to climb

They're both brilliant red
Your juices and mine
But today I'm the victor
Because you're in a pie.

The Muse

My senses are more aware.
I see art in nightfall.
I hear music in daybreak.
My dormant, fickle fertility
Is suddenly, amazingly in full production.

The wind carries honeysuckle from the next yard.

I use my hands, my vision, to
Draw, immortalize all I see.

The sun and I share a wink.
He knows what I've been up to —
Enriching his kingdom
Life love colors blood earth breath rain.

In the evening, the moon
Rocks me to sleep, with her secret songs.
I will sing them to all who listen.

I can touch the treetops
See faces, elephants in clouds.
I grow with April daffodils.

The wind carries honeysuckle from the next yard.
I hear deer rustle in the woods.

I can write.

I see a robin in search of nesting.

 I have found mine,
And will fill it with my creation.

SUSAN SHULTZ

The Wooden Spoon

Amidst the peeler,
Forgotten pitter,
Against your worth
Ladle's a quitter.

You may be clean
But you respond –
My meals, your memory
My porous wand.

You are a weapon,
You are a muse.
You've been a part
Of cauldrons, stews.

I'll take your splinters
You take the heat,
Our give and take
Makes meals complete.

When plastic burns
And dull's the knife —

My wooden spoon
Brings roots and life.

The Hangover

The dark dancing man
Is spinning in my eyes
In black and white.

The dark monster man
Is dancing in my head
In black and red.

"Come on," he said
"Get out of bed.
There's lots to do.
A drink for me.
A drink for you.

Or maybe two?"

As he poked through
The times I've bled
Kept in my head.

He shook my brain
Till every pain.

So neatly bound
So tightly wound

Came tumbling free —
He clapped with glee
"What's this?" Said he
"It's ecstasy!"

"A drink for me
A drink for you
Or maybe three."

He splashed in pools
Of ancient tears.
He laughed at buried
Childhood fears.
 He pulled each stitch and nail and knot
Until my heart
Was pulled apart.

And when his fun
Was finally done
Gave me a wink
"How bout a drink?
What's one more?
Or is it four?"

And in the morning sun
My eyes are red and white
 The room spins —

The dark man laughs —
 And lies in wait for night.

Petals

We hide our heart
Our caged target —
It's beat the base
From which we started.

A flower grows
Each day so bold —
It never hides
It's color's soul.

The bee that borrows
Ensures tomorrows.
The nectar it lacks
Will always come back.

A daisy undresses
Without human stresses —
Reminds us that giving
Won't impede our living.

Let's open our petals
So our life can be touched —
If we don't – we might dry up
To be next year's mulch.

Broken

They replaced my pitcher,
With cracks in composition.
Though I've not complained,
Nor expressed imposition.

I traced its cracks
After finding discarded.
I understood,
Having been broken hearted.

It has cradled my flowers.
I embraced its sharp teeth.
We both have parts missing,
To which blooms bring relief.

My pitcher, it leaks –
But it stays front and center.
Together our splits
Let love out, but not enter.

My pitcher tries hard
With mending and missed shards.

It's ok to be broken –
Takes one to know one.

My Gift

The martyr is silent
As the rocks
Are piled mercilessly
Upon his quivering chest
no cry escapes
I only give you what I can

The good servant
Reaps the harvest
The sun rays like whips
Raise welts
Upon his blistered, beaten back
— Still he reaps
Until night fall
I only offer you what I have

My tears,
Containing smaller worlds
Of shattered hopes
Of sleepless dreams driven by
The relentless ambition to change
The endless cycles
— Set in motion by
The prehistoric magistrate of organization
You cannot have what is lost.

SUSAN SHULTZ

September

Where the summer leaves
The residue of sweat
On nature's children
Breathless from the rain
Tousled from the heat
Weary for the cooling hand
Of autumn on their forehead

The lullaby of leaves
Crisp and ready
To fall into reluctant sleep
Are cradled in the arms
Of the gold sky

They sing sweetly
Of what is to come

Just Another Day at Work

For William

I stand at the edge
Of this emptiness
This enormous,
Whistling void,
Dizzy with its Delirious depth.

Your tears
In my eyes
Your ache
In my heart.
I can't take your burden
Can I explain Your pain?

As I leave you —
Your many rooms
Magnified loss
The lack of laughter —

Can silence echo?
Does grief seek out grief?
The ghost I can't unsee
May give us relief

His eyes, they still haunt me
My fear must not daunt me.
I'm shackled to sorrow —
To a suffering shadow —

Inspire me to be brave —
Help me.
HELP me.
There's lives
We can save.

To Gram

If I could understand
Only one moment
Of life that's been accomplished
Encompassed by your shining eyes —

Once arms, stronger,
Lending me support
As I toddled through
To embody your strength —

But can I hope to ever be as wise
Or as synonymous
With what it is
To love.

Recipe

Start with a good stock.

Boost your bones,
Foster fiber,
Instill integrity.

Make a roux.

Enhance your essence.
Distill your dedication,
Whisk your worth.

Simmer your soul

Only
Invite ingredients
To foster your flavor,
Carry your character,
Tease your taste.

Don't

Salt away your sweetness,
Sugar down your strength,
Pepper over your personality,
Over muddle your makeup.

Cook on low heat
For a lifetime.

Taste.
Test.

Because once the cooking's done
You're at a table for one.

Don't let it cool
Congealed and casted off.

Don't over heat
Because burning's just bitter.

But stock
Is the start —

Without it
You have no depth
No heart.

The Staten Island Ferry, post 9/11

I step out into
The city's version of fresh air
Away the stray remnants
Of sunlight
That mix with the night
To form dusk
Deceive me.

The last drops of day can be tasted
In their pinks and yellows.

In this light, the sidewalks
Almost seem clean
Until a downwind
Assails my nose
With the unidentifiable.

Boarding, we are cattle.
I become more intimate
With my unshaven neighbor
Than he deserves.

I climb the steps
Seat myself on an open bench
Overlooking the Hudson.
The reflection of the evening sky

Creates a mirror that belies
The polluted monster it hides.

Startled, as always, by the foghorn,
I watch the Manhattan skyline
Thrusting out its many chests
Though they number less —

All bravado despite this loss —
I mentally genuflect.

As my little boat floats slowly home,
The skyline grows smaller —
As darkness settles,
Making edges — and absences — indiscernible.

Skipping Rocks

My life is a narrative of quick fixes.

The minimum payment.
The splicing of the cassette tape
The candle in place of electricity

The book read aloud in the car
to mask my own thoughts

The $5 in my gas tank
To just get where I need to go and

My life is the fleeting laugh
to drown the tears.
My life is saying I'm sorry for what others did wrong.
My life is fake flowers, colorful and without fragrance.

My life is a joke to change the subject.
the foundation in the wrong color
on sale at CVS to hide the wrinkled years.

My life is clothes that don't fit
and the pile put aside
for when i just know they will again.

My life is wiping off the bathroom sink

with my dirty laundry
So it 'looks' clean.

It's sleeping in my clothes because
I don't have time to change.

My life is splurging for the horror movie
so I forget about folding the laundry
My life is telling everyone, "Don't worry about it,"
When I never stop worrying.

Blinking back the tears,
because I'm just sneezing —
It really doesn't hurt.

It's the over the counter in the place of
a needed prescription.
It's keeping the lights off in the shower
so I can't see the truth.

It's pretending to love the darkness
When I'm really afraid of the light.
Not effacing, it is self-eviscerating.

My life is a blindfold,
over eyes closed,
and letting go of your hand,
before you can do it first.

My life is a minimum payment.
It's piling smiles on the pain I've buried.

to make you feel better.

My life is the silence
used to disguise heartbreak.
It's a changed subject.
It's a funny anecdote.

My days are a series of skipped rocks
across life's surface,
I can't swim,
I don't want to know how deep the water is.

It's quick fixes.
It's choking on my anger.
A map trail of broken spine leading to another concession.
It's zero investment.

My life is constantly apologizing for what's been done to me,
Just so I can breathe another day.
I've got this.
It's on me.
I understand.
Don't worry about it.

I'm a candle in the darkness.
Vulnerable to even a glance,
 My life is a narrative of quick fixes.
As I surrender
to nothing, and again, ask,
 "But how are you?"

Break the Sky

The young forget that only creatures die
The child dreams his own immensity
And circles violet hazed intensity
His only driving need to break the sky

But later on, the boy can't see as high
And his ambitions aims for smaller spheres
Surrenders to his aching mortal fears
Afraid to fall, afraid to break the sky

And now as the old man prepares to die
The dreams return to taunt him with his fate
So violet burst and stars now separate
Allowing them at least to break the sky

The soul forgets that only mortals die
It's final driving need to break the sky.

For Mom

Remember when we used to spar?
I really wish you would.
There were some times I'd get annoyed
Because of how you are

But now I only miss the way
You were so who you were.
I long for days we'd draw our swords.
Today's Excalibur.

My gauntlet lies in dust these days.
You're somewhere deep inside.
Are you afraid?
Can somehow you seek a safe space to hide?

These thoughts - they keep me up at night.
But where to spill them to?
Because you are now lost away —
or else I'd share with you.

The way you'd break a kneecap for us all,
I miss the most.
Don't worry, mom, we've got you —
our turn now to stand at post.

15

We took the bus home, sat in regular spots
Walked home cutting through the local graveyard
We'd wave our way through the family plots
Picking up the pace as the sky grew dark

We never noticed the names on the stones, or the ages
Of those who were under our feet.
Not a thought that the pathway we took was through bones
Our chatter was light — our laughter sweet.

By the park in the trees
A waterfall splashed and we'd stop to watch
As if it were new.
We'd lean over as far as we possibly could
To hold spitting contests
To spoil the view.

A cold day in March, as winter held on
The shock was like lightning as a false hope of dawn.

You were gone.

My childhood,
innocence,
irreparably torn.

And then I would notice

The names on the stones.
And the ages of those resting under my feet.
Every day, I would lie six feet over your bones
And imagine I could still could still hear your heart beat.

And every March brings,
Though it's been many years —

Your laughter
Your memory

My waterfall tears.

Beer

Lifelong dreams
Swirl and dance
Within a golden reflection

The distorted image
Swims before me

Visible in the half-light
Of these lonely candles

My only choice —
To swallow myself.

Effigy

An effigy
What's left of me
Stones
Bones

Can you see
What can't be free?
What used to be?
Intensity
Integrity
Vitality

How can it be —
This fallacy?
My weaponry —
Desensitize
Use a disguise.

Will weakness be
my legacy?
Or is there still
A chance for me?

But
Risk-restricted
Self-convicted
Hope, evicted

Loss, predicted
I fear to see
And fail to be.

Evoke in me
Integrity
Resiliency

Don't bury me
Save effigies

This
will
not
be

My eulogy.

The Race

For Susan

Bang.

The starting gun
Wakes me from my sleep
Slowly I begin to run,
Breathing slow and deep.

Sleeping, I was safe and warm,
But a runner breathes alone.
I try to look beyond the storm
And catch a glimpse of home.

Turn my head, see a face,
Eyes straight, head held high —
Struggles, tries to keep the pace.
She's not as strong as I.

I pause a moment, slow my gait —
She says, "Go on, I'm all right.
If only I can look straight ahead,
I'll make it through the night."

Hours ago, I made my start.
Night stretches silky black.
Light footsteps thunder behind my heart.

I keep on looking back.

Now we reach a steep dark hill.
I know that if she makes the top,
She'll make it all the way — she will!
Then the footsteps behind my stop.

Turning, I see a crumpled heap,
She, who held her head high.
She whispers, "The hill is too damn steep."
I answer, "You must try."

Pour some water on her face,
Help her stand, her body aching.
Slowly, we resume the race,
Side by side, the rules forsaken.

Strong wind comes, she falls with a cry,
and says, "Just leave me here."
Lift her up, point to the sky,
"See the sun? We're almost there."

Smile down, the storm is calm,
Her body still as the ocean deep,
Speak softly, lightly touch her arm,
Try to wake her from her sleep.

Her eyes don't flutter.

No wind blows.

So the silence tells what I already know.

The sun burns my face
And I long to erase
All the times and moments before.
In exchange for a minute —
Oh, what I'd say in it!
For an hour or two hours more.

But the moment is gone —
And I am alone.

Still miles to go until I reach home.

I'll continue to run,
Caring not who has won.

Only remembering the sound of the gun.

Bang.

Susan Shultz is a published novelist and poet, a long-time award winning journalist and mom of two, who lives in Connecticut. When she is not offering a taxi service to her two teenagers, she loves to cook, garden, read, write and watch horror movies.

CPSIA information can be obtained
at www.ICGtesting.com
Printed in the USA
BVHW091201181022
649721BV00006B/465